Bi

Phil Moser can be summed up in two words: biblical and practical. He is a master at applying the Scriptures to everyday issues in such a way that people walk away with lives changed.

KEVIN O'BRIAN
Pastor, Ocean City Baptist Church

Phil Moser has done an admirable job of identifying spiritual principles and then applying them to daily life. I commend this work both to those struggling with their daily walk, and to those counselors who are seeking additional tools.

DR. JOHN MACARTHUR
Pastor-Teacher, Grace Community Church
President, The Master's Seminary

Hats off to Phil Moser for helping us navigate through life's most challenging issues in a clearly biblical way. The thing I like about these booklets is that they are forged by a pastor who has successfully wrestled through these issues with his flock, and thankfully he now shares them with the church at large.

DR. JOE STOWELL
President, Cornerstone University

It has been a high privilege to know Phil Moser for more than 20 years. He is one of today's most gifted communicators; possessing an unusual ability to deliver biblical truth in an intensely personal and practical way. Our guests and students rate him a perennial favorite. I can give no higher recommendation for your next conference or speaking opportunity.

DON LOUGH
Executive Director, Word of Life Fellowship

Pastor Phil's writing reflects a deep commitment to helping individuals both understand and obey God's Word in their daily life. As an experienced counselor he realizes that just teaching the truth is not enough; people need help on the practical steps of disciplining themselves for the purpose of godliness. I commend this combination of exposition, call to obedience and "how-to."

RANDY PATTEN
Director of Training and Advancement
Association of Certified Biblical Counselors

As an educator, Phil Moser is distinctively gifted. His pedagogical skill enables him to clearly explain very difficult concepts in understandable language that all learners can grasp. Audiences would greatly benefit by his teaching.

CAROL A. SHARP, PH.D.
Served as Dean of the College of Education 2002-2012
Rowan University, Glassboro, New Jersey

I have been greatly encouraged by Phil's teaching. When I listen to him, I always walk away with more. More knowledge, more insight, more understanding, more hope. He's my go-to-guy when I have questions about the Bible or Christian living.

MICHAEL BOGGS
Singer-Songwriter
Winner of Multiple Dove Awards

The Biblical Strategies materials have been a big plus for our adult classes. With the inclusion of the memory verse packs and accountability study guides, the materials lend themselves readily to the discipleship process.

STEVE WILLOUGHBY
Pastor, First Baptist Church of Patchogue, New York

Dead-End Desire

biblical strategies for overcoming self-pity

Phil Moser

Dead –End Desires: biblical strategies for defeating self-pity

Published by Biblical Strategies.
Distributed by Send the Light.

Visit our Web site: www.biblicalstrategies.com.

Credits:
Cover Art: gracewaymedia.com, Gary Lizzi
Copy Editors: Wes Brown, Justin Carlton

Contributions:
A special thanks to Jack Klose for his thought provoking questions that are a part of every accountability plan/study guide.

Note: You may download a free accountability plan/study guide for *Dead-End Desire* by visiting biblicalstrategies.com. Choose the resource tab to print the guide and other tools.

CONTENTS

IDENTIFYING
DEAD-END ROADS

S EVERAL years ago the road I traveled home at the end of the day was washed out in one of those torrential rains that come around every hundred years. For nearly ten years this had been my route home, but now there was a barrier placed at the half way point. My habitual commute ended with a dead-end. It took them two years to repair that road. For two years my commute included an extra five miles nearly every day, because I kept forgetting the road was out until I saw the barricade. I'd turn around and drive out the same way I'd come in, telling myself that I wouldn't make the same mistake tomorrow.

My route home during that time parallels my struggle with self-pity. Even though I know it is a road leading nowhere, I instinctively choose it as if I have no other option. Self-pity is best defined as the preoccupation with yourself because your hopes, desires, or expectations have not been realized. It is unproductive and destructive to all relationships. From time to time, I still find myself on that all-too-familiar road, unable to remember how I got there until I see that barricade and realize I'm approaching self-pity's dead-end.

In the Scriptures we discover God's thoughts on self-pity through his conversations with biblical characters. Three in particular are worth noting: Cain, Moses, and Jonah. Each encounter reveals God's warnings for those on the dead-end road of self-pity. They also provide God's gracious solutions for how to return to a life of productivity. A careful study of the biblical characters reveals several common features in their battles with self-pity:

- It followed a mountain-top experience
- It revealed a prideful desire for another's approval
- It intensified when they ran from responsibility
- It grew in the discontented heart
- It increased when they compared themselves to others
- It fueled various forms of anger
- It led to despair

While some of the features were similar, there were marked differences in the final outcomes. Moses was successful at defeating self-pity and went on to live a productive life. Cain and Jonah were not; they simply would not stop thinking about themselves.

Self-pity is sometimes mistaken for humility, but it is actually a prideful response, even though it may not feel that way to us or appear that way to others. C.S. Lewis shows us the nature of genuine humility when he writes, "True humility is not thinking less of yourself, it is thinking of yourself less."[1] Like the facade on a rotting structure, self-pity is a false humility. True humility is so sharply focused on others that it will sacrifice itself completely for another.

This is clearly the pattern Jesus demonstrated for us. When the disciples were arguing about who should be the greatest, Jesus saw it as an opportunity to talk about the cross. He says, "For even the Son of Man came not to be served, but to serve and to give his life a ransom for many."[2] Jesus encourages us to do the same.[3]

While the Father teaches us how to think,[4] and the Son exemplifies for us what to do,[5] it is the Holy Spirit's power that actually makes change possible.[6] He empowers us to make God-honoring choices.[7] As we cooperate with him, those daily choices will become daily habits, and lasting change will follow. This is what it means to walk in the Spirit.[8]

Perhaps you know self-pity firsthand. Your circumstances seem overwhelming. Negative thoughts consume your thinking. Feeling sorry for yourself has become a way of life. While you used to battle temptation, lately you can't find the energy to try. You compare yourself to others and come up short. No matter where you start, all roads seem to lead to self-pity's dead-end. This booklet was written with you in mind. It is intended to get you off a road that leads nowhere and to put you back on the road God wants for you. Three simple truths will serve as your signposts: think like God thinks, do what Jesus did, and follow where the Spirit leads.

THINK LIKE GOD THINKS
The Dialogue with Cain:
Self-Pity Interprets Instruction as Rejection

THERE was one field with two altars. There were two brothers with one intention: to offer a sacrifice to God.[9] Cain knew he hadn't brought his best stuff, but he figured God would be okay with it. He'd felt a twinge of conscience when he kept the better portion for himself. Still, he reasoned, *if you have to give to a God you can't see, maybe he can't see what you give*.[10]

As he lifted the sheaves onto the altar, he smelled mildew, the first signs of decay in the offering he was giving. Abel came to the field with his firstborn ram in tow. Suddenly Cain felt a bit nervous, like one underdressed for a special occasion. For a moment, he wished he had brought something better. Abel slaughtered the ram and placed it on the altar. He lifted his blood-stained hands and began to pray. Cain watched, acutely aware of the inadequacy of his own sacrifice. A streak of light crossed the evening sky accompanied by a crash of thunder. Fire fell from heaven, consuming Abel's sacrifice.[11] His offering accepted, Abel bowed humbly and retreated from the altar.

As Abel's sacrifice burned on the adjacent altar, Cain noticed an incessant buzzing around his. Drawn by the smell of mildew, flies were beginning to gather on the rotting grain; today's eggs would bring tomorrow's maggots. Cain's face fell. He was embarrassed. The rejection that should have brought humility stirred a different emotion: self-pity. Thoughts began to gather like the flies on his sacrifice: *Had he not fulfilled his worship obligation? Had he not* given something? *Who was God to reject his worship and accept Abel's?* He went home dejected and sulked through the night.

Returning to the field the next morning, he noticed Abel's altar. Pure white ash was all that remained of the offering. He glanced at his own. The sheaves of grain were moving unnaturally, as if they had come to life. He drew closer and discovered the cause. The eggs had hatched, and the maggots were feeding on his second best. Holy fire had taken Abel's offering; Cain's was fit only for worms. The feeling of rejection was palpable. Self-pity was fertile soil for his anger; resentment showed on his face.

It was then that God spoke: "Why are you angry? And why has your face fallen? If you do well, will you not be accepted?"[12] *God made it sound so easy,* Cain thought. *But it doesn't feel easy.* He didn't want acceptance on God's terms; he wanted it on his own. He glanced at Abel's altar again, the ash gently blowing, a reminder of God's approval. While God's tone was instructive, Cain heard it as rejection. His thoughts shifted quickly to his brother. *Maybe it was Abel's fault he felt this way. If only he hadn't brought the perfect ram.* His anger grew quickly into jealousy, and murderous rage followed close behind.[13]

The desires God had told him to control grew stronger, pressing hard on his will.[14] Cain made up his mind. He called Abel to the field. Naïve of his brother's intentions, Abel came. As the brothers neared the two altars, Cain drew back, stooping down to pick up a rock. Self-pity, anger, and jealousy merged together, energizing his intention. In the open field before him, Cain saw two things: his altar with its worm-infested sacrifice and the back of his brother's head. When he was done, there was blood on his hands. There was blood on the ground, and God was calling his name again.

W E DON'T know much about Cain's life or his relationship with his brother prior to the murder. We do know that he was the firstborn son and that his mother saw his birth as significant. Notice the text: "Now Adam knew Eve his wife, and she conceived and bore Cain, saying, 'I have gotten a man with the help of the LORD.' And again, she bore his brother Abel."[15] Some Bible scholars have inferred from Eve's words that she believed she had given birth to the Messiah.[16] Perhaps she thought that Cain was the one who could right her wrongs and strike Satan's head.[17] Cain sounds like the Hebrew word for *gotten*. In stark contrast, Abel's name comes from the word that means air, breath, meaningless, nothing.[18]

Imagine those introductions to future generations. *This is my son who is a gift from God, and this is my son who means nothing.* You would think that the brother who would feel sorry for himself would be Abel, yet the opposite is true. This offers hope to those whose home life has been less than perfect. You are not a product of your environment. God grants you the freedom to consider your past, interpret the details, and make choices about how you will live differently. Abel did this. Perhaps he developed humility from his mother's bias towards his brother; we can't be certain. But we do know this: Abel trusted the Lord[19] and offered the best that he had as an act of worship.[20]

Cain, on the other hand, refused to receive instruction. He interpreted it as rejection. If you grew up in an environment that was free from criticism, you may be prone to do the same. My parents were very encouraging and rarely critical. Because of that, I was relatively confident in whatever I attempted, but I have tended to overreact to criticism. In cases where I should have learned from criticism and sought to see it as constructive,[21] I've been prone to feel sorry for myself that I received it. All too often I've welcomed self-pity as a familiar friend when I should have been seeking to change in response to the instruction that was given. This appears to be Cain's weakness as well. God graciously offered instruction in spite of Cain's careless sacrifice, but he wasn't receiving it. Notice the text from Genesis 4:3-7:

> In the course of time Cain brought to the LORD an offering of the fruit of the ground, and Abel also brought of the firstborn of his flock and of their fat portions. And the LORD had regard for Abel and his offering, but for Cain and his offering he had no regard. So Cain was very angry, and his face fell. The LORD said to Cain, "Why are you angry, and why has your face fallen? If you do well, will you not be accepted? And if you do not do well, sin is crouching at the door. Its desire is for you, but you must rule over it."[22]

Cain wears his self-pity for all to see. God addresses his attitude with a question, a solution, and a warning.

The Question

Throughout the Scriptures, God asks questions for which he knows the answers. He uses these questions to move the listener towards change. As a friend of mine once shared, "A question stirs the conscience, but an accusation hardens the will."[23] This was God's approach with Cain when he asked, "Why are you angry and why has your face fallen?"[24] The use of the "why" question implies that Cain had a choice. God was stirring Cain's conscience when he asked why. He could choose not to be angry if he would humbly obey.[25]

Our ability to make the right choice is captured in the English word "responsible," a word we often use without considering its meaning. We are response-able—that is, we are able to choose the right response as we depend upon the Lord and follow his leading. I recognize that it doesn't often feel this way. Self-pity consumes our thoughts. The ensuing emotions drain the strength from our desire to change. Before long it feels like self-pity happens to us, that we have no choice but to feel this way. The question God posed to Cain is a good reminder for each of us. Ask yourself, "Why am I choosing to respond in this way?"

God's question points out that Cain chose to feel sorry for himself. He was not the victim of his emotions or circumstances. Self-pity, while an enslaving habit, was still a choice. Paul confirms this in the book of Romans:

> Don't you realize that you become the slave of whatever you choose to obey? You can be a slave to sin, which leads to death, or you can choose to obey God, which leads to righteous living.[26]

In God's question we find a liberating truth: you don't have to be embroiled in self-pity—you choose to be.

The Solution

When Cain's initial sacrifice was not accepted, God offered him a solution. We find this solution in God's second question: "If you do well, will you not be accepted?"[27] Thankfully, we serve a God of second chances.[28] This is especially evident when you study those who struggled with self-pity. God often shows them mercy. Perhaps this is because his attribute of mercy is closely linked to the word pity. The Greek scholar W.E. Vine explains:

> *Mercy* is the outward manifestation of *pity*; it assumes need on the part of him who receives it, and resources adequate to meet the need on the part of him who shows it. It is used of God, who is rich in mercy." [emphasis added][29]

God looks upon our situation and pities us. He openly expresses his pity when he shows us mercy. This is why self-pity is a woefully inadequate comforter. Notice Vine's description again: "Mercy . . . assumes need on the part of him who receives it, and resources adequate to meet the need on the part of him who shows it." We are in need of a resource outside of ourselves; we can't be both the receiver and the giver. God, who is rich in mercy, is the giver. In the case of Cain, he gave a second opportunity. He said, "If you do well, will you not be accepted?" In his graciousness, God was saying: *Go ahead, Cain. Try again. I won't hold this poor sacrifice against you. Bring me another. I'll accept it.*

But Cain wasn't interested in second chances. Self-pity rarely is. He had chosen to interpret instruction as rejection, and a do-over didn't seem viable. Self-pity whispered, *You'll only be rejected again. Just sit tight and claim you already tried.* The problem Cain had with God's solution is that he didn't really want to try again. A second chance on God's part, meant a second effort on his, and that was something he was unwilling to do. Rather than receive God's instruction as constructive and work towards change, it was easier to interpret it as rejection and claim that any change would still be unsatisfactory.

Laziness is insidious; it takes many forms. A friend was kind of enough to point this out to me in my personal struggle with self-pity. When I would face a conflict, I was quick to take the blame. Self-pity would settle in, my attitude would degenerate, and I would angrily proclaim to myself (and at times to others), "I just can't get anything right!" I shared this with my friend thinking he would give me sympathy. Instead, he gave me something far better – the truth. "Phil," he said, "you beat yourself up first, so that no one else will. As long as you can avoid hearing what they have to say, you can remain lazy; and change will be unnecessary." My friend's words were life-altering. While I had not considered myself a lazy person, I had to agree with his analysis. Taking the blame quickly was my default mechanism to avoid further conflict, 'avoid' being the key word. I was unwilling to put in the extra effort necessary for growth and change.

This was Cain's error and one we easily make as well. Accepting God's solution meant humbling himself and trying again. It was easier to stay on the dead-end road and blame God for the fact that he had to walk it alone. W h e n we feel rejection, we ought to ask: *Why was I rejected? Is there something I can do differently? Is there a change I need to make for the next time?* Cain ignored these questions. Still, self-pity could not relieve those persistent feelings of rejection. To ease them he would need to find someone else to blame. His brother was the most likely candidate. Self-pity is rarely self-contained, and it usually saves its greatest destruction for those closest to us. God knew this danger was lurking, so he issued a warning.

The Warning

Cain doesn't know where self-pity is taking him, but God does. He warns Cain, "If you do not do well, sin is crouching at the door. Its desire is for you, but you must rule over it."[30] Self-pity is the doorway to a host of other sins. No one chooses to sin without thinking that their actions are justified. As Cain continued walking in self-pity, he grew increasingly comfortable with his angry emotions. As his anger intensified, his intentions to murder his brother seemed more reasonable. Self-pity left him defenseless against an onslaught of strong sinful desires. The more that he imagined the fulfillment of those desires, the more justified his actions seemed.

Desire in and of itself is not wrong. In the Bible, the object of the desire determines whether it's right or wrong.[31] For instance, a husband should desire to spend quality time with his wife. That would be a good desire. But if that same husband desired to spend quality time with another man's wife, that would be a sinful desire. The word desire is used in both sentences, but changing the object of the desire changes the meaning of the word.

So what was the object of Cain's desire? Cain wanted acceptance, but he wanted that acceptance on his terms, not God's. The author of Hebrews makes it clear that Cain didn't bring his best, but Cain's anger revealed that he believed that it should be good enough.[32]

Our response to an unmet desire often reveals the nature of the desire. Nicholas Ellen writes,

> So when we act in ungodly ways in response to not getting what we want, we expose what we treasure above God and His will. For instance when we reject others, withdraw, stop serving . . . we expose that we value something above obedience to God and love to others.[33]

Whenever we dwell upon an unmet sinful desire, it will grow stronger. At the same time, our resolve to do what is right will weaken.[34] This is why God described Cain's sin as "crouching at the door."[35]

When I was in 9th grade, I had a classmate who had a 90-pound terrier that had a reputation for sinking his teeth into intruders. The dog had only one weakness: it feared water. My friends and I would run through the backyard with a water pistol as our only means of protection. The dog would slowly advance with his eyes focused on his prey, but at the first sign of the water he would back off. When he would begin that low-crouched crawl in your direction, you knew that his desire was for you. But being overconfident fifteen-year-olds, the more often we escaped the backyard unscathed, the less attentive we were to the very real danger. Then came the day my water pistol jammed. I can still remember the sudden realization that the dog was going to bite me. My back was against the wall, there was no time to run, he was coming, and he was coming fast. In my impudence I miscalculated the danger, and 35 years later my knee still bears the scar to prove it.

Cain miscalculated the danger too. He clung to self-pity too long; his angry desires overwhelmed him. God, in his mercy, saw Cain's pain and reached down to help. But Cain was so lost in himself that he perceived God's instruction as rejection. He ignored God's questions, refused God's solution, and didn't heed God's warning. If you don't want to be bitten by the dog, get out of his back yard. If you don't want to fall into more destructive sins, steer clear of self-pity. Sin is crouching at the door, and its desire is for you.

THE DIALOGUE WITH MOSES
Self Pity Distorts Your View of Reality

M OSES stood at the door of his tent; he shook his head, weary of the Israelites' griping.[36] *Is God as worn out by this as I am? They're thirsty. They're tired. They don't like what's for dinner. They miss Egypt. This job is impossible, and the people are even more so.* With a heavy sigh, he looked at the column of fire suspended in the night sky above the camp. For 40 years he had written their laws, resolved their conflicts, led them into battle, pointed them to God, and listened to them complain. They had become proficient at it. Most of them would grumble all the way to the grave. Tonight they sounded like whining children. Their chorus of complaints filled the valley.[37] He knew God's wrath was coming. It had happened before,[38] and it would happen again.[39]

This time, though, something stirred inside of Moses. The seed of self-pity took root and began to grow. Moses was agitated; he felt like a nurse maid unable to quiet the crying babies. He hated that image, but it was how he felt when the people wouldn't stop complaining. Before he knew it, he lifted his eyes towards heaven and added his cynicism to the rising chorus. *Why are you treating me this way? What did I ever do to you to deserve this? Did I conceive them? Was I their mother? So why dump the responsibility of this people on me? Why tell me to carry them around like a nursing mother, carry them all the way to the land you promised to their ancestors? Where am I supposed to get meat for all these people who are whining to me, 'Give us meat; we want meat.' I can't do this by myself—it's too much, all these people. If this is how you intend to treat me, do me a favor and* kill me. I've seen enough; I've had enough. Let me out of here.[40]

God heard his servant, and he answered. *Moses, call 70 elders; I will share your burden with them, and I will serve the people the meat they desire. I will feed them meat for a month.*[41] To Moses, God's answer seemed like too little too late. Self-pity had taken root in his heart. His will felt strangely unwilling to change; his anger barred the door of escape. It felt right to think only of himself. Critical of the people's complaints, Moses couldn't seem to stop his own. Before he realized it, he started to tell God what to do. *Have you counted these people, Lord? You really think you can keep the buffet line coming for 30 days? There aren't enough fish in the sea to feed this bunch of whiners.*[42] God answered: *Moses, has my arm been shortened since I did all those miracles in Egypt? You remember them, don't you? You were given a front row seat then. Take one now; I have some dinner to prepare.*

S ELF-PITY distorts your view of the past, the present, and what God can do with your future. Moses was not exempt from succumbing to dead-end desires; don't assume you will be. By the time we get to the events of Numbers 11, the Israelites had developed a fairly consistent pattern of complaining. God had already changed the names of two of their campsites,[43] and he would change the name of three more[44] to immortalize their negative spirit.

Can you imagine if your home town was named *Quarreling with God*[45] or *Rebellious Craving.*[46] Likewise, God had punished the grumblers. There were new grave markers at those locations when the people moved on.[47] In the 11th chapter of Numbers the complaining spirit is so pervasive that it affects even Moses.[48] Although he usually handled complaints with grace and humility,[49] even he struggled with feeling sorry for himself under such pressure.

(1) A Distorted View of the Past: Your Memory is Selective

I used to wonder how the Israelites, who had been eyewitnesses to many of God's miracles, could develop such a complaining spirit. Then one day I read the Apostle Paul's comment to the Corinthians:

> Now these things happened to them as an example, but they were written down for our instruction. [...] Therefore let anyone who thinks that he stands take heed lest he fall.[50]

We don't want to say, "I would never do that." We need to train our minds to say, "I could sin in that way; that's why I want to receive instruction humbly."

To overlook God's awesome work in our past and develop a complaining spirit, we need only be selective in the way that we remember the past. We see this tendency in the Numbers 11 narrative:

> Now the people became like those who complain of adversity in the hearing of the LORD; and when the LORD heard it, His anger was kindled . . . the sons of Israel wept again and said, "Who will give us meat to eat? *We remember the fish which we used to eat free in Egypt.*" [emphasis added][51]

Did they just say they remembered eating *for free*? Talk about revisionist history. Were they not the slaves of Egyptian tyrants for 420 years? Weren't the final years in Egypt unbearably difficult?[52] How could they forget how bad their past was? The same way they forgot how good God was. Their memory was selective.

We learn a valuable lesson from the Israelites, easily missed in the first reading: our desires generate selective memories.[53] Like an intentional case of Alzheimer's, we choose to leave things out of the story so that we might get what we want.[54] In this case, the Israelites wanted meat instead of manna. That, in and of itself, would not have been sinful, except that God was the one serving up the manna. Furthermore, God had a far greater lesson he wanted them to learn when they hungered in the wilderness. Moses points to it nearly 40 years later when he instructed the next generation.

> And you shall remember the whole way that the LORD your God has led you . . . testing you to know what was in your heart. [...] And he humbled you and let you hunger and fed you with manna, which you did not know, nor did your fathers know, that he might make you know that man does not live by bread alone, but man lives by every word that comes from the mouth of the LORD.[55]

God wanted them to turn to him when they were hungry. He was the provider of every good and perfect gift.[56] In God alone they would find their fulfillment, but the Israelites were convinced that a good steak would suffice. The purpose of our circumstances (especially the difficult ones) is always greater dependence on the Lord.[57]

The people assumed that their less than desirable circumstances were cause to complain. Actually, they were an opportunity to depend more fully on God. Perhaps you're shaking your head in disbelief, unable to understand how the Israelites were never able to grasp this truth. Careful. They weren't the only ones to struggle with a selective memory. I know that same struggle, and I bet you do too.

We get so focused on what we don't have, that it's easy to forget what we do have. If I promised you the thing you really wanted right now, you might be willing to tweak your past a bit to get it. Just like the Israelites, our desires rewrite the events of our past. We too, can fall prey to a selective memory.

This past year my wife Kym started keeping a diary of the ways God had worked on our behalf. As the kids chimed in around the dinner table one night, I suddenly realized that I had already forgotten some of the things that I had praised God for just a few months earlier (go to page 63 to start your own praise journal). Selective memory is like a scalpel, cutting out your recollection of God's work in your past. Once you've begun to forget, a complaining spirit isn't far behind.

(2) A Distorted View of the Present: You Feel Alone

Self-pity isolates you from your most meaningful relationships. You tell yourself you want to be left alone, but then you feel sorry for yourself when no one shows an interest. You say you would rather work by yourself, but then, discontented, you envy those who work with others. Before long you become so self-consumed that you're convinced you're alone even though you're not.

Because self-pity is so closely tied to your emotions[58] it's easy to shift the basis of your belief from God's promises to your feelings. This is a subtle shift in thinking, but the ramifications are catastrophic. For instance, if your confidence is in the promises of God, those promises anchor you to God's unchanging character.[59] However, if you determine your truth-base from your feelings, truth becomes unstable, shifting like the currents of the sea.

Our feelings are influenced by both external and internal forces. External forces derive from our particular circumstances and might include things like our friends and acquaintances, the economy, traffic, or even the weather. But those forces aren't alone; there are also internal forces that press upon our emotions. Perhaps you are hungry, tired, bitter, guilty, or hormonal. Both the external and internal forces can send us tossing like an unanchored ship in a storm. This is why we determine truth from the promises of God, not how we feel at the moment.

The story of Moses teaches us how easy it is to forget this truth. Moses knew the promises of God; he had recorded them with his own hand. But when he chose not to rehearse them to himself, he became even more deeply mired in self-pity.

Trust the Promise, not your Feelings.

You're not Alone.

At the beginning of Moses' ministry, God promised: "I will be with you."[60] Forty years later, at his retirement from service, we read, "And there has not arisen a prophet . . . like Moses, whom the LORD knew face to face."[61] From the beginning of his ministry to the end, God promised to be with him, and he kept his promise. God never left Moses alone. However, in the middle of his ministry, wearied by the complaints of the people, Moses released the anchor. He forgot God's promise and leaned into his feelings. Moses said to the LORD,

> Why have I not found favor in your sight, that you lay the burden of all this people on me? . . . *I am not able to carry all this people alone; the burden is too heavy for me* [emphasis added].[62]

Moses wasn't really alone, but he really felt that way. God's promise had not failed; Moses just didn't believe it any longer. It is significant that Moses speaks of being alone not as a feeling, but as a substantiated fact. If Moses had chosen God's promise as his basis for truth, he could have endured those strong external and internal forces without succumbing to self-pity. Instead, he chose his feelings.

Years ago I memorized a poem that has helped clarify this idea. I come back to it often when I'm tempted to let my feelings lead. As you read, interpret *fact* as *God's promises*.

Three men were walking on a wall,

Feeling, Faith, and Fact.

Feeling had an awful fall,

And Faith was taken back,

But Fact remained and pulled Faith though

And Faith brought Feeling too.

If Moses hadn't cut himself free from the anchor of God's promise, perhaps his prayer might have sounded something like this: *God, I feel really alone right now. The people are complaining, they don't like what you're serving, and they insist that I do something about it. But even though I feel alone, I will cling to your promise that "you will always be with me." Please strengthen me so that I don't waver in my belief.*

For me, the prayer that focuses on God's promise brings clarity. It is my self-pity that brings confusion. God made the same promise to us he made to Moses. In the New Testament we read, "'I will never leave you nor forsake you.' So we can confidently say, 'The Lord is my helper; I will not fear; what can man do to me?'"[63] God's promise doesn't waver, but my feelings do.

Apply the Promise in Spite of your Feelings.

Don't Act like You're Alone.

Because Moses felt like he was alone, he cried out, "The burden is too heavy for me."[64] God never told him to carry the burden alone. Moses forgot that in all of those past miracles he was only the instrument, not the source. It was never God's intention that we should labor without his strength. When we attempt to do things on our own, the burden will get heavy quickly. When we choose God's way, we can find hope even in the most difficult of circumstances. 1 Corinthians 10:13 reminds us of this truth. *The New Living Translation* renders it this way:

> And God is faithful. He will not allow the temptation to be more than you can stand. When you are tempted, he will show you a way out so that you can endure.[65]

This truth alone is a self-pity stopper. You are not alone; God is faithful. The trial, even though it may be devastating, is not more than you can bear. He will show you a way out so that you can endure.

My wife and I have a dear friend whose husband rejected her for another woman, hiding the truth from her for over a year. During that time, she experienced discouragement and despair, fear and anger, loneliness and rejection. The marriage would ultimately end in divorce, but her loneliness continued. For her, the loneliness was most debilitating in the morning. Sometimes she didn't even feel like she had the strength to get out of bed. Rather than succumb to the loneliness, she devised a plan. Before she went to bed, she would open three Bibles and place one on her nightstand, dresser, and bathroom vanity. When she awoke, her eyes would fall on the open Bible on the nightstand, and she would read until she found the strength to get out of bed. It was three steps to the next Bible on her dresser. With both hands on the dresser, she would again lean into the Word, repeating God's promises to her that she would not be alone in her trial. Eventually she would make it to her bathroom vanity where the third Bible was open. In remembering that God would never leave her,[66] she would find the strength to begin her day.

Here's the truth: we were not meant to be alone,[67] and God has made great sacrifices to insure that we don't have to be.[68]

(3) A Distorted View of God: You Think He's Like You

Moses truly believed he was on his own. Because he couldn't imagine a way that he could feed all of those people, he assumed that God wasn't up to the task either. Moses said,

> The people among whom I am number six hundred thousand on foot,[69] and you have said, 'I will give them meat, that they may eat a whole month!' Shall flocks and herds be slaughtered for them, and be enough for them? Or shall all the fish of the sea be gathered together for them, and be enough for them? [70]

Did Moses, the instrument through which God had done his wonders, just tell God something can't be done? Moses figured if he couldn't do it, God couldn't do it either. God corrected him with a great deal more patience than I would have offered. God himself picks up the dialogue: "Is the LORD's hand shortened? Now you shall see whether my word will come true for you or not."[71] It's like God is telling Moses, *Do not assume I can only do what you can do.* With the words, "shall see" God speaks of a future only he knows; he puts Moses back in his place. *Moses, you can't see the future, but I can. You are not like me; you just think you are.*

Ultimately we embrace self-pity not only because our perspective of self is too large, but because our view of God is too small. Just like Moses, when we struggle with self-pity it can ultimately be traced to a pride problem. We think of ourselves too often and/or too highly. Mark Twain once commented, "God created man in his own image and man, being a gentleman, returned the favor." It's true. We have a tendency to think that God is constrained by our human limitations.[72] This is a distorted view of God, not one developed from a focus on theology, but one that grows out of our limited understanding of what we believe is possible. Songwriter William McDowell reminds us,

> You are not a God created by human hands,
> You are not a God dependent on any mortal man.
> You are not a God in need of anything we can give,
> You are God. That's just the way it is.[73]

Assume God's Responsibilities and You'll Neglect Your Own.

One of the common themes I've observed as a pastor is that people often fail to do what they should do because they're trying to do what only God can do. None of us are equipped to carry out God's role, but that doesn't keep us from trying. For instance:

- God sees the future. We can't see it, so we *worry* instead.[74]

- God knows a person's inner desires and intentions. We can't know them, so we develop a *judgmental spirit*, questioning their motives.[75]

- God can change a heart; we can't, but we try. We seek

30

to *control and manipulate* others through our words and emotional responses.[76]

When we attempt to do God's job, we end up falling down on our own. Look back at the emphasized words in the previous points. God told us not to worry,[77] not to judge another's heart,[78] and not to control and manipulate others.[79] When we attempt to do what only God can do, we fail to do what he asks us to do. The Bible teaches that we are totally inadequate to carry out God's responsibilities.[80] Just like Moses, we not only do them poorly, but complain because the burden is too great to bear. This is prime territory for self-pity to grow, as God's dialogue with Moses reveals. So how do we overcome this tendency? By trusting God with those less than desirable circumstances and believing that he can accomplish something purposeful through them.[81]

This was a truth that carried Joseph through betrayal, slavery, false accusations, and nearly ten years in prison.[82] At the conclusion of his story, he reminds his brothers, "As for you, you meant evil against me, but God meant it for good, to bring it about that many people should be kept alive, as they are today."[83] In spite of his suffering, Joseph had grown in contentment. He didn't need his brothers' approval to feel successful. He found it easy to love them and forgive. He didn't need pleasant surroundings or positive conditions. It's not our circumstances that make us prone to self-pity, it's our dissatisfaction with those circumstances. Self-pity takes root in the soil of discontentment.

Self-pity distorts your view of life. Through a selective memory, it will alter your view of the past; by causing you to think you're all alone, it will shape your view of the present; and it will raise doubts about God's ability to work in

31

your future. Where self-pity is, hopelessness abounds. Yet, God is not limited by what we believe. While Moses' faith was weak, it had not always been, nor would it always be. God would redeem the moment, and Moses would trust God again. Moses made it off self-pity's dead-end road. He reviewed the promises of God and made decisions in accordance with what he believed, not simply what he felt.

THE DIALOGUE WITH JONAH
Self Pity has an Aversion to Grace

JONAH winced under the noonday heat.[84] Ever since his ride in the belly of the sea creature, his skin was extra-sensitive to the sun's rays. The temperature wasn't the only thing rising, though; so was Jonah's temper. The more he rehearsed the events of the past 40 days, the more justified his bitterness seemed. After all, he'd done what God had asked, so what happened to God's plan of action? He thought about the Ninevites again, his blood pressure rising. He raised his fist to heaven and shouted. *What's wrong with you God? How long does it take you to destroy a city? Send some angels or something. I did exactly what you told me. I promised them your judgment, so let's get on with it! Give these people what they deserve!*

As if to accentuate the silence of heaven, the only movement in the noon sky was a vulture rising effortlessly higher. Jonah shook his head in disgust and slumped down against a rock. His chin hit his chest, and he dozed. When he awoke, he noticed the beginnings of small plant behind him. A few days later the ground was covered in shadow, the vine's branches reached over the rock. *Finally!* Jonah said to himself. *Some shade for the faithful prophet.* He turned his gaze back towards heaven and picked up the one-way conversation. *That's what I'm talking about, God. Giving people what they deserve. When I did wrong, you put me in the belly of a whale. But when I did what you asked, you paid with shade.* He permitted himself a smile. *Not the wages I was hoping for, but it's a start.* The shade temporarily cooled his internal resentment.

The next morning he awakened to beads of perspiration gathering on his forehead. He turned to look at the plant that had provided comfort the day before. Its leaves were shriveled, its branches sagging. *What happened to you?* Jonah spoke to the plant. His eyes caught a movement at the base of the vine. A worm quickly retreated into the hole it had made. *Are you kidding me!* Jonah was talking to the sky again. *What kind of games are you playing God? I want my plant back, and I want it back now. You owe me.*

As if in direct response to Jonah's anger, an eastern wind stirred the desert sand, quickly whipping it into a frenzy. Jonah shielded his eyes, unwilling to turn back to the west as the sand beat against his face. Like a child forced to lift his chin and look into his parent's eyes, the desert sand turned Jonah's head. The blowing sand allowed only one place to fill his field of vision: Nineveh. He stared at the city whose destruction he desired. The east wind with its swirling sand insisted his gaze remain upon God's gracious redemption of a city once condemned. Jonah glowered, unwilling to let his anger subside. God's grace poured out on the people he despised.

The rushing wind subsided, and the sound of voices singing rose from the valley below. It was a song of grace coming from the city that understood the meaning of the word. Jonah knew the song, but he refused to join in. Still, he couldn't keep the lyrics from running through this head: *The Lord is good, his mercy endures forever, his faithfulness to all generations.*[85]

JONAH introduces us to the most dangerous element of self-pity: its aversion to grace. The Bible uses the word often. The Greek word for grace (*charis*) occurs over 155 times in the New Testament. Its Hebrew equivalent (*hen*) occurs 70 times in the Old Testament. Both Testaments carry the same warning: you will not see your need for grace unless you come in humility.[86]

On the surface, self-pity and humility appear to be similar, so it's easy to miss self-pity's rejection of grace. For instance, the individual struggling with self-pity and the one practicing humility both lack confidence for a given task, but only the humble of spirit will actually seek help.[87] The one encumbered with self-pity will choose to feel sorry for himself rather than humbly asking for guidance.

Because humility is unconcerned with receiving glory, it will naturally seek a source of strength outside of itself.[88] Self-pity, on the other hand, is overly concerned with the approval of others.[89] Rather than reveal its sense of inadequacy, it will simply not try. Our fear of failure often stems from a fear of what others will think of us if we fail. Self-pity is a deceptive comforter, encouraging us not to pursue our true potential instead of simply admitting we need help. This explains why most men that surrender to self-pity will rarely ask for help regardless of the type of struggle they are facing.[90] It isn't humility that insists on going it alone, it's pride. While self-pity can be mistaken for humility, it is actually motivated by the prideful protection of one's self-interest. It is the natural response of a prideful spirit, not a humble one. This is also why self-pity has an aversion to grace: you cannot see your need for grace unless you come in humility.[91] This is even clearer when you consider Jonah's response to God's actions.

For the longest time I couldn't understand Jonah. God saved his life when he was thrown overboard,[92] gave him a second chance,[93] and even provided for his comfort.[94] It seemed absurd that he was willing to receive grace for himself but unwilling to extend it to others. Then one day it occurred to me that Jonah didn't see these events in his life as expressions of grace, but rather, because of his pride, things he deserved from God. Part of the reason Jonah found joy in the plant was because he believed he deserved its shade. He didn't see it as a gift from God, which would explain his anger when the plant died. It was his right, he reasoned, and it had been unfairly taken from him.

Contrast Jonah's response to his loss of comfort with that of Job, who not only lost his comfort but his family and wealth, too. When Job was tried, he replied: "The Lord gave, and the Lord has taken away; blessed be the name of the Lord."[95] Job understood the grace of God, and saw himself as an undeserving recipient.[96] Jonah would never have said that; he believed you got what you deserved. Thus, he was angry when Nineveh was not destroyed. He believed the Ninevites should have gotten what they deserved, but God, in his grace, stayed his judgment because the city humbly repented.[97]

Self-pity says: I am angry. I deserve to have my desires met.

Jonah's unrestrained desires appear throughout the story. He didn't want to go to Nineveh, so he boarded a ship going the opposite direction.[98] He was asleep in the hold when he should have been helping save the ship.[99] The destruction of Nineveh was his ultimate desire, which is why he was exceedingly angry when God withheld judgment.[100] But Jonah's problem was greater than a few unrestrained desires. He actually believed that the things he desired were things that he deserved. Self-pity says *I believe that something I desire and deserve is being unfairly kept from me.*

We struggle with self-pity for the same reason that Jonah did. We have unmet desires, and we believe we deserve to have them realized. Your unmet desires might include things like love from your spouse, respect from your teenagers, or gratitude from a fellow worker. These are not necessarily bad desires, but when you begin to believe you deserve them, pride is leading you down self-pity's road. When those desires go unmet, just like Jonah, you will become angry.[101] This is why self-pity has an aversion to grace. It doesn't want a gift. It pouts, believing it has not yet received what it has earned. Perhaps you're sensing the freedom of this truth. I encourage you to embrace it. Stop waiting for what you think you deserve. Learn to be thankful for what God, in his grace, has given.

Humility says: I am grateful. I didn't receive what I justly deserved.

This is most clearly communicated in the gospel message. We deserved death for sinful offenses before a holy God. But God, in his grace, gave his own Son to die in our place that we might receive the free gift of eternal life. We cannot earn it, and we do not deserve it. It can only be received as a gift of grace. Pride will reject this offer of help, but humility will accept it. Humility says, *I believe that something I deserved, but didn't desire, was graciously kept from me.* In contrast to Jonah's self-pity, note the apostle Paul's humility. He believed that what he deserved was the judgment of God for his past actions; nonetheless, God graciously forgave him. His humility allowed him to transparently acknowledge his past failures, regardless of the social status of the listener. Before King Agrippa he states,

I myself was convinced that I ought to do many things

in opposing the name of Jesus of Nazareth. And I did so in Jerusalem. I not only locked up many of the saints in prison after receiving authority from the chief priests, but when they were put to death I cast my vote against them. And I punished them often in all the synagogues and tried to make them blaspheme, and in raging fury against them I persecuted them even to foreign cities.[102]

In his letter to the Corinthians he states the same:

For I am the least of the apostles, unworthy to be called an apostle, because I persecuted the church of God. But by the grace of God I am what I am, and his grace toward me was not in vain. On the contrary, I worked harder than any of them, though it was not I, but the grace of God that is with me.[103]

Grace is the word Paul chose to describe the fact that God kept from him the judgment that he rightly deserved.

Whereas Jonah in his pride believed he deserved the things he desired, Paul in his humility expressed gratitude that he did not receive what he rightly deserved. Humility prepares us to receive grace; self-pity cannot. Perhaps this is why Jonah's story ends so abruptly. It is intended to remind the reader that, unless we humble ourselves, there is no hope of change. Self-pity will hold you captive.

DO WHAT JESUS DID

T HE BIBLE teaches that though Jesus lived his entire earthly life within the intrinsic limitations of humanity, he never sinned.[104] Therefore, he provides us with the perfect case study. What did he think about? What choices did he make? How did he control his emotions? Answering these questions well is very instructive for those of us who are attempting to walk in his footsteps.[105] The circumstances Jesus faced would have caused the strongest of individuals to feel sorry for themselves. Consider:

- His own family didn't believe his message and desired his destruction[106]
- When he prayed, he didn't always get the answer he desired[107]
- He was betrayed by Judas, a professing friend[108]
- He was falsely accused and unjustly tried[109]
- His most devoted followers first slept through, then ran away, in his greatest hour of need[110]
- He faced the injustice of the official (Pilate) who was in place for his protection

Through it all, Jesus expressed pity for others, but he never indulged in feeling sorry for himself.[111] When we examine his responses, we gain a greater understanding of how we can avoid self-pity. Jesus' focus was Godward. He dwelled upon God's love, sought God's will, and lived for God's glory. His responses stand in stark contrast to the attitudes of Cain, Moses and Jonah all of whom were consumed with self.

(1) Dwell Upon the Love of God

When we feel we aren't loved, particularly by those closest to us, we are susceptible to self-pity. Perhaps others may have treated you harshly, spoken unkindly, or judged you unfairly. It's easy to feel unloved in these situations.

When it comes to defining love, our culture clearly puts the emphasis on what we feel. Statements like: *I feel like I'm falling in love,* and *I don't feel like I love you anymore* reflect this error.[112] Our inclination to interpret love by how we feel affects both how we think about others and how we think they think about us. This is one of the reasons that, in spite of all the biblical evidence that God loves us, some still choose to believe that he does not. They do not *feel* that he loves them.[113]

When feelings become your foundation, you are in a catch-22; you don't like the way you feel, but you have chosen to let your feelings lead the way. Something will need to change if you are to break this endless cycle. The cycle is broken once you give love a biblical definition, not simply an emotional one. The Bible sees love as more of an action than an emotion. Consider Paul's words to the Corinthians:

> Love is patient and kind; love does not envy or boast; it is not arrogant or rude. It does not insist on its own way; it is not irritable or resentful; it does not rejoice at wrongdoing, but rejoices with the truth. Love bears all things, believes all things, hopes all things, endures all things. Love never ends.[114]

The Greeks had five separate words to describe our one English word for love, so we should expect some ambiguity when we try to describe the word with our limited vocabulary. Of the five possible words, the one the New Testament writers most often chose was the Greek word *agape*.

This word communicates a love of choice, commitment, and promise as opposed to an emotionally charged decision.[115] The Bible teaches that we are to love one another in spite of how we feel. God doesn't ask us to do what he himself has not done. The apostle Paul reminded the first-century Romans that while they were still God's enemies, he showed his love to them through the death of his Son.[116] True love will make similar sacrifices, regardless of how one feels. Because self-pity is driven by our feelings, a feelings-based love will be unable to defeat it. To overcome self-pity, you will need to focus on a commitment-based love.

This is precisely what the Father provided for Jesus in the darkest hour of his life. Jesus struggled emotionally in that final week of his life, but there is no record that he doubted his Father's love.[117] Rather, he seems to have interpreted everything through his unshakable confidence in his Father's commitment. Six words reflect his security: *as the Father has loved me.*[118] The historical context of those words should not be overlooked. Nearly a third of John's gospel is devoted to the final hours of Jesus' life before he is crucified. Humanity's hatred and cruelty is directed at Jesus in those moments. His disciples are selfish; he is betrayed by a close friend; his trial is a travesty of justice; he is mocked, beaten, and spit upon. One might expect self-pity to run rampant given those circumstances. If we were in Jesus' place, we might choose six different words: *why is this happening to me* or *this is how you treat me*? Not so with Jesus. In the middle of it all he states: *as the Father has loved me.* Jesus remembers the Father's commitment to love him and his unchanging character that backs it up.[119] Self-pity can't bring its discontentment to the heart that is secure in the Father's love.

Jesus' six words of security are followed by five words of sacrifice: *As the Father has loved me, so I have loved you.*[120] When we dwell upon the way that God loves us, we find inspiration to love others in spite of their treatment of us. Later in the conversation Jesus would qualify it further: "Greater love has no one than this, that someone lay down his life for his friends."[121] By looking to God's love, we take our eyes off our self long enough to give our attention to others. In fact, this was Jesus' final charge to his disciples just hours before he was nailed to the cross: "This is my commandment, that you love one another *as I have loved you.*"[122] Jesus had a commitment-based love just like his Father, and he encouraged his followers do the same.

Have you ever wondered how Jonah's story might have ended differently if he had focused on God's love and not followed his feelings of self-pity? Perhaps there would have been a 5th chapter – one that spoke of Jonah rejoicing in his enemies' repentance and giving praise for God's gracious dealings with mankind. How might your life be different if you began to focus on the love of God? What if each time you began to feel sorry for yourself you reflected upon the love of God instead? When self-pity settles in, only a strong dose of God's love will drive it out.

(2) Seek the Will of God

When man was created, he was placed in a garden. That garden was perfect in every way, and only one tree was off-limits. Adam and Eve were asked to submit their wills to their Creator by not eating from the tree of the knowledge of good and evil. All was well until their desires were awakened.[123] Then, for the first time, they felt the tension between their will and God's will. Maybe they'd never considered their choices before. Maybe, just for a moment, they felt pity for themselves because God had denied them the fruit from the one tree. We may never know, but what we do know is this: God wanted something for them, but they wanted something else for themselves. They chose what they wanted and stepped outside of God's will for the first time. The consequences for their choice were disastrous.[124]

On the night before his crucifixion, Jesus returned to a garden. He was no stranger to the garden of Gethsemane, having frequented it with his disciples.[125] But this time was different. In the Garden of Eden, the will of man had been tempted, and man had chosen independence over surrender. In the Garden of Gethsemane, the will of man would be tempted again, but this time the desire for God's will would overpower personal desires. Jesus expressed this in prayer with the words: "Nevertheless, not my will, but yours be done." He had progressed in his understanding of, and obedience to, his Father's will.[126] In the midst of intensely difficult circumstances that would cause even the strongest of men or women to pity themselves, Jesus held such feelings at bay by focusing on the will of God and pursuing it with abandon. Jesus submitted to the will of God because he trusted the character of God. Three aspects of God's character will increase our confidence to seek his will over our own: his wisdom, his love, and his power.

God's Wisdom

Living with suffering is hard work. It's easy to lose your focus. Once your focus is disoriented, it becomes difficult to avoid self-pity. Suffering can come in many forms, not all of them physical. Our mind struggles with harsh and critical statements that seem unjustified. Our emotions vacillate between confusion, anger, and grief when circumstances in our life seem to contradict the hand of a loving God. When the apostle Peter heard of the suffering that Jesus would have to endure, he tried to protect Jesus. He said, "Far be it from you, Lord! This shall never happen to you."[127] Jesus' answer was quick and to the point: "Get behind me, Satan! You are a hindrance to me. For you are not setting your mind on the things of God, but the things of man."[128]

Jesus focused on a specific aspect of the character of God—his wisdom. God thinks differently than man thinks. The wisdom of man is short-sighted and pragmatic,[129] but God's wisdom is eternal and directed purposefully. The ability to focus on the character of God—not the wisdom of man—is a quality that Jesus developed, and he exercised it most fully in the garden of Gethsemane.[130]

God's Love

As the suffering of the cross drew near, Jesus asked if there might be another way. Mark recounts it this way: "And he said, 'Abba, Father, all things are possible for you. Remove this cup from me. Yet not what I will, but what you will.'"[131] *Abba* is a family term.[132] It might best be rendered in the language of our day as "Daddy." When my kids want the quickest access to my heart, this is how they address me. It's the term that every dad knows—like they're saying, "Dad, I know you love me." Jesus is clinging to the character of his Father's love. He finds resolve for submitting to his Father's will by reflecting upon his Father's love. Believing that God is all-wise means that God *knows* what is best for us; believing that he is all-loving means that he *wants* what is best for us. With gut-wrenching suffering on the horizon, Jesus didn't question his Father's love.

God's Power

Immediately following Jesus' affirmation of his Father's love, he affirms his Father's power. He says, "all things are possible for you." This is not the first time Jesus has used those words. He had acknowledged God's power on other occasions with the very same phrase.[133] But in the Garden of Gethsemane, his belief is tested at the highest level. Does he really believe that the Father has the power to act if he should choose? Yes, he does. This is expressed in his final words from the cross, "Father, into your hands I commit my Spirit."[134] Having breathed his last, he reveals a complete dependence. Jesus believes his all-powerful Father will bring about his resurrection.[135] Jesus embraces the will of God by focusing on the character of God. He does not question his Father's wisdom, love, or power. This enables him to surrender his will to his Father's.

One of my seminary professors who made a profound impact on my life was Dr. Fred Barshaw. Prior to becoming a pastor, Fred served as a public school teacher. Gifted in understanding the learning process, he received the esteemed "Teacher of the Year" award for the state of California. Fred's strength was his application of the Word to real life situations, and I was drawn to the unique ways he found to communicate. During my final year, Fred began his battle with cancer. I graduated and headed into ministry on the other side of the continent. Several years later, I was developing material for a class I was teaching, when I realized my lay out and presentation looked strikingly familiar. I went to my filing cabinet, pulled out my notes from one of Fred's classes, placed them next to my own, and immediately recognized the similarity. It almost looked like I had plagiarized. Having not intended to do so, I realized I was teaching just like my teacher. I picked up the phone and called Fred, wanting to communicate my deep sense of gratitude for his investment in my life. Cancer had taken its toll. He was short of breath and spoke with a hoarse whisper. Because he was so weak I expressed my appreciation quickly, then asked how I could pray for him. There was a long pause and then the words: "pray that I would be faithful to the end." A remarkable request considering the amount of pain and suffering he was enduring. I prayed that way. Within a month Fred Barshaw died, faithful to the end.

Our response to suffering can take one of two roads. Either we can seek to do God's will by dwelling upon his character, or we can focus on the difficulty of our circumstances. If we choose the latter, self-pity won't be far behind. Fred Barshaw did what Jesus did. To the very end he sought the will of God, and that's what we should do too.

(3) Live for the Glory of God

In self-pity we take our eyes off of God and focus them on ourselves—our circumstances, our difficulties, our weaknesses. It shouldn't surprise us, therefore, that we aren't making decisions with the glory of God in view. The final week of Jesus' life is instructive. Ultimately it would be his commitment to the glory of God that guided his thoughts away from the trap of self-pity.

When You're Frightened, Live for His Glory.

In the final week of his life, Jesus spoke with great transparency of his soul's emotional condition. On Tuesday of the Passion Week, one of his disciples brought to him a group of non-believers. The teaching moment prompted

Jesus to speak about his death. In so doing, he opened up a window onto his soul. Jesus spoke of a grain of wheat that falls into the ground and dies that it might bring forth much fruit.[136] The conversation reminded him of his own impending death. He responded with the phrase, "Now is my soul troubled." There is a sense of violence to the word "troubled" that eludes our English language. The Greek root word *tarasso* is used elsewhere in the Bible to reveal one's condition at the loss of a loved one.[137]

As a pastor, I have been, on more than one occasion, the bearer of the news that a loved one has died. I have heard uncontrollable wailing. I have seen sheer terror in the eyes of a young boy at the news of his father's death. I have seen the body shake uncontrollably as emotions reject restraint. When a parent loses a child, sometimes the soul refuses to be comforted. I have heard of people that responded to this kind of news with vomiting or by losing consciousness. This is the very word that Jesus chose to describe how his soul felt with only a few days between himself and the cross. The fear moved him to prayer—even though a crowd had gathered—and that prayer reveals his focus. He says,

> Now is my soul troubled (*tarasso*). And what shall I say? "Father, save me from this hour"? But for this purpose I have come to this hour. Father, glorify your name.[138]

With overwhelming fear rising in his soul, Jesus riveted his attention on the glory of God. It was his greatest desire even if it would mean his death.

When You're Disappointed, Live for His Glory.

Occasionally in my ministry I've known the disappointment of someone who walked away from what I'd taught them. Perhaps in your life you've experienced a similar event. Consider the disappointment that Jesus faced in the final week of his life. On the night before his crucifixion, Jesus gathered the disciples for a final evening of fellowship and instruction. Luke recorded that Jesus actually looked forward to their final hours together.[139] Over dinner, a debate broke out among the disciples over who was to be the greatest. They were in the mood to bicker, but in no mood to serve.

Imagine the situation from Jesus' perspective: three years of selfless ministry, his sacrificial death less than twenty-four hours away, and still they're arguing. That's enough to push anyone into the self-pity chasm. But look at his response:

> Jesus . . . rose from supper. He laid aside his outer garments, and taking a towel, tied it around his waist. Then he poured water into a basin and began to wash the disciples' feet and to wipe them with the towel that was wrapped around him.[140]

Remarkable. Where we would see an opportunity for self-pity, Jesus saw an opportunity for service. Jesus did this without fanfare or attention; he took no credit for his actions when the last foot was washed. He was as much a servant as he was a host. There was no sense of entitlement; he chose a spirit of humility instead. With that humility came the desire to pursue his Father's glory and not his own. The apostle Paul captured it this way,

> Have this mind among yourselves, which is yours in Christ Jesus, who, though he was in the form of God, did not count equality with God a thing to be grasped, but emptied himself, by taking the form of a servant, being born in the likeness of men. And being found in

human form, he humbled himself by becoming obedi-
ent to the point of death, even death on a cross.[141]
When we don't feel the need to get the glory, we are more
prone to serve. And when we give the glory to God, we are
most like Jesus.

FOLLOW AS THE SPIRIT LEADS

SELF-PITY lures us into isolation. When we're feeling sorry for ourselves, we want to be alone but then wonder why no one wants to be with us. We withdraw from others. Even when a close friend or family member pursues us we tend to back away. The more we feel alone, the more we withdraw, and the cycle of isolation continues.

Jesus promised the disciples that he would send the Holy Spirit so they wouldn't be alone. He said, "I tell you the truth: 'It is to your advantage that I go away, for if I do not go away, the Helper will not come to you. But if I go, I will send him to you.'"[142] Jesus chose a great word to describe the third member of the Trinity. He referred to the Spirit as "the Helper." English translators captured this word in other ways: advocate, intercessor, counselor, comforter.

The Greek word being translated "helper" is *parakletos*. It is comprised of two ideas: *para*, which means "along side," and *kaleo*, which means "to call forth." For someone who feels alone or isolated, this offers encouragement. Your condition is not determined by your feelings. The Holy Spirit is nearby and available to guide, comfort, and empower you when you call him.

Because he is readily available, the Bible describes this relationship as walking in the Spirit. Our part, as we walk together,[143] is to discover his direction,[144] be satisfied with his comfort,[145] and trust his power to be sufficient to bring about real change.[146] While this new pattern is challenging for someone who battles self-pity, it is possible.[147]

(1) The Spirit and the Word: Discovering His Direction

Jesus taught that the Holy Spirit would both disclose truth and guide us in it.[148] The Holy Spirit does this as we: (1) study the Word for discovery; (2) memorize the Word for instant retrieval; and (3) apply the Word for change.[149] The Holy Spirit was the unseen agent behind the writing of the Scripture.[150] The apostle Peter declared: "For no prophecy was ever produced by the will of man, but men spoke from God as they were carried along by the Holy Spirit."[151]

Study the Word for Discovery

The Spirit was not only active in the writing of Scripture, he also plays an active role in our study and interpretation. The apostle John recorded,

> You have received the Holy Spirit, and he lives within you, so you don't need anyone to teach you what is true. For the Spirit teaches you everything you need to know, and what he teaches is true—it is not a lie.[152]

When we read and study the Word, the Holy Spirit is the teacher, and you and I are the students. When we come to the Word of God, we come humbly—as learners.

It is always surprising to me how few of us know the pertinent passages of Scripture or have systematically memorized the key Bible verses that pertain to our struggle. To press the teacher-student metaphor further, it does not matter how masterful the teacher is if the student is unwilling to study. Cain's life demonstrated that someone struggling with self-pity will not receive instruction well. If you are to be led by the Spirit, and self-pity is your challenge, you will need to persevere in your study of God's Word. A 28-day Bible reading schedule is provided on page

63. The passages were selected with Jesus' path to victory in mind. For further study, we encourage you to try the accountability plan/study guide. You may download and print a free copy at www.biblicalstrategies.com.

Memorize the Word for Instant Retrieval

When Jesus was tempted by Satan in the wilderness, he responded with the memorized Word.[153] He didn't have a scroll, a notebook, or a smart phone with a Bible app. Instead, he had diligently placed the verses in his memory so that he could retrieve them at a moment's notice. In 20 years of pastoral counseling on a wide variety of challenges, I can count on one hand those who had memorized biblical passages before they came to me. Scripture memory may be the most underdeveloped resource for those in need of help. Temptation is often fast and furious; your ability to retrieve the appropriate Scripture quickly is your best means of defense.

It is impossible to retrieve what you have never memorized. To aid you in getting started, you will find 20 biblical passages pertaining to self-pity on pages 66-67. To expose temptation's deception, we memorize ten verses in the lie/truth formula. To weaken temptation's appeal, we learn ten verses about the character of God and the nature of the gospel. The *Scripture Retrieval System*, which provides verse cards with helpful commentary, is available at www.biblicalstrategies.com.

Apply the Word for Change

The Scripture warns us that we have deceived ourselves when we are hearers of the Word but not doers.[154] Once you've studied and memorized key passages, you must apply them at the time of temptation if you hope to change. Paul gave practical steps to do this in his letter to the Galatians. He wrote, "But I say, walk by the Spirit, and you will not gratify the desires of the flesh."[155] Two lists follow that command: the works of the flesh and the fruit of the Spirit. Imagine yourself at a crossroads. There are only two paths from which to choose. One is marked "the works of the flesh;" the other, "the fruit of the Spirit." Walking in the Spirit means whenever you are tempted, you take a step of faith toward the *fruit of the Spirit* list and away from the *works of the flesh* list. For instance, you choose patience, not fits of anger.[156] You move towards peace, not dissension.[157] You settle your thoughts on loving others, not sensual pleasure.[158]

Applying the Word for change is what happens every time you make that choice at the crossroads. Often your feelings will be drawing you one way, but by faith you will need to choose the other. Eventually the new habit will become instinctive, and you will keep in step with the Spirit more naturally. In the beginning, developing this habit will take a concentrated effort. Examine the two lists found in Galatians 5:19-23, then ask yourself what patterns now form your daily habits.

(2) The Spirit and Prayer: Being Satisfied with His Comfort

Because self-pity leads towards isolation, it's difficult to find comfort when you're hurting. You feel all alone. You wonder if anyone knows or cares. Actually, the Spirit of God does both. The old King James Version used the term "comforter" to describe the Spirit's work.[159] This is most evident in how the Holy Spirit intercedes on our behalf.

The Scripture records,

> Likewise the Spirit helps us in our weakness. For we do not know what to pray for as we ought, but the Spirit himself intercedes for us with groanings too deep for words. And he who searches hearts knows what is the mind of the Spirit, because the Spirit intercedes for the saints according to the will of God.[160]

When we looked at the lives of Cain, Moses, and Jonah in their struggle with self-pity, we found them in conversation with God. Although their words lacked the proper attitude and content, at least they were praying. When we struggle with feelings of self-pity, we are likely to pray with a complaining spirit, too. Remember, self-pity grows in the soil of a prideful heart; you will need to come to the Lord with a spirit of humility if you hope to be heard.[161] One of the ways we can do this is to allow our prayers to be shaped by one of the 650 prayers in the Bible.[162] These prayers provide valuable patterns that help us word our personal prayer.[163] Take the key elements of a biblical prayer and build your praise, confession, and requests around it. You will find several recommended prayer patterns on pages 60-62.

(3) The Spirit and Power: Walking in His Strength

Feelings of self-pity can come on quickly and are often stronger than we would have expected. Fortunately, we don't battle them in our own strength. The Spirit empowers us to choose rightly. Paul builds his argument for depending upon the Holy Spirit's strength instead of our own by giving an example of the Holy

Spirit's power:

> If the Spirit of him who raised Jesus from the dead dwells in you, he who raised Christ Jesus from the dead will also give life to your mortal bodies through his Spirit who dwells in you.[164]

So this all-powerful Spirit indwells us. But how? Corrie ten Boom, the Dutch Christian who, along with her family, helped the Jews escape during the Holocaust and then suffered for years in the Ravensbruck prison, used to offer this insight:

> I have a glove here in my hand. The glove cannot do anything by itself, but when my hand is in it, it can do many things. True, it is not the glove, but my hand in the glove that acts. We are gloves. It is the Holy Spirit in us who is the hand, who does the job. We have to make room for the hand so that every finger is filled.[165]

It is hard to imagine the kind of power that raised Jesus from the dead dwelling within us, but the clear teaching of Scripture affirms this truth. We don't have to surrender to the feelings of self-pity, no matter how strong. The one who indwells us is more powerful than our feelings, and he strengthens us to make new choices. Because self-pity has become habitual, change is only possible by making new choices that are enabled by the power of the Spirit.

Getting Off
the Dead-End Road

M Y FAVORITE building in Washington D.C. is the Library of Congress. Upon its completion in 1897, it was the most costly library ever built. Congress commissioned 40 artists and sculptors to prepare pieces for its corridors. If you visit, be careful not to get left behind. There are 838 miles of bookshelves housing over 150 million items.[166] In the center of the library is the reading room. Eight giant marble columns support the gold plated dome that peaks at the Torch of Learning 195 feet above the ground. The upper balconies support 16 bronze statues. The statues commemorate those whose lives shaped history: Beethoven. Michelangelo. Shakespeare. Homer. Newton. Plato. Visitors walk out to that balcony because it provides the best view of the reading room.

On a recent visit, my family and I ascended the stairs and stepped onto the balcony. The view took my breath away: such expanse, beauty, and solitude. I turned to my left and looked into the stern face of Moses. There he was, holding the Ten Commandments, staring down upon the readers in the largest library in the world. I thought to myself: *Moses made the top 16.* He was still exerting his influence 3,500 years after his death.

I imagined what his life might have been like if he had never made it off self-pity's dead-end road. What if he had felt sorry for himself because he was left in a basket as a child? What if he had never recovered from the shame of taking another's life? What if he had fallen into self-pity when he made that abrupt career change from Egyptian dignitary to humble shepherd? What if he had lamented that life had passed him by when he turned 80?[167] Would he have ever made it back to Egypt? Would he have been used by God to bring about one of the greatest deliverances in the history of the world?

Self-pity has derailed many who *could* have been used by God, but who instead succumbed to their feelings and, as a result, withdrew their names from the list of history changers. They sat it out, feeling sorry for themselves. Don't be one of them. If you find that you have succumbed to that dead-end desire, do what Jesus did: dwell upon the love of God, seek the will of God, and live for the glory of God. It's not too late. There's a lot to do, and you may be just the one to do it.

How to Apply What You've Learned

The discovery of new truths is the beginning of change, but discovery by itself cannot accomplish real change. To do that, you will need to replace your old habits with new ones, your old ideas with more accurate ones, and your old thoughts with more biblical ones. The final pages of this booklet are dedicated to helping you establish those new habits. Prayer, Scripture and the Holy Spirit were the divine resources that Jesus used, and those same resources are available to you and me today.

(1) Prayer

For those who have a pattern of self-pity, changing their pattern of prayer is essential. The following pages offer two different prayer patterns, and help on developing a praise journal.

(2) Scripture

Jesus was victorious over self-pity as he dwelt upon the love of God, the will of God and the glory of God. To deepen your understanding of these essentials, I have provided 28 days of Bible readings in these areas. If you desire to go further, you will find study questions accompanying each passage at biblicalstrategies.com. To aid with Scripture retrieval, we have provided 20 biblical passages to memorize that apply directly to self-pity.

(3) The Spirit

Dependence on the Spirit is essential for defeating self-pity. Developing new habits by walking in the Spirit is the means through which we express that daily dependence.

The 10 Minute Prayer Pattern: PRAY

The *PRAY* acrostic is a memory device for prayer. It can be as short as a few minutes, or may include more time as God leads. PRAY stands for Praise, Repent, Ask, and Yield.

(1) Praise

At the beginning of prayer, praise the *who*, *what*, and *why* of God. Praise him for *who* he is by reflecting upon his character. When you remember *what* he's done, you are meditating on his works. Finally, remember the *why* of God. He is motivated by his steadfast love towards us (Psa. 100:5).

(2) Repent

Once you've thought about what God has done, you can move easily to what you haven't done. Repentance takes place when we remember our failures and turn from them. A humble confession in prayer reveals a dependence on the Spirit in order to be restored to God. True repentance includes my actions and attitudes (Phil. 2:5).

(3) Ask

Jesus taught us to *ask* of God, and Paul gave us a great prayer list (see Col. 1:9-12). The spiritual nature of the prayers of Scriptures are helpful in praying for yourself and others.

(4) Yield

Jesus grew to the point where he could say, "Not my will but yours be done." Yielding your desires (as hard as that may initially be) is an essential element of prayer. Once you've made known your requests, make sure you surrender your desires.

Nehemiah's Prayer Pattern

The Old Testament saint Nehemiah found himself in the kind of situation that would lead many into self-pity. His fellow Israelites had been stripped from their land and taken away into slavery; he served the King of Babylon as the cupbearer. His job was to taste the king's food to see if someone had tried to poison the king. He was living over 600 miles away from his hometown of Jerusalem when he received the news that his hometown had been devastated. He was deeply moved, weeping for days. Both his circumstances and his emotional response could have brought on a bout of self-pity, but Nehemiah chose to pray. His prayer provides a balanced pattern for how we ought to pray to stave off self-pity tendencies.

(1) The First Focus: Praise & Thanksgiving

We typically don't think of praising God when our circumstances are difficult and we are distraught emotionally, yet Nehemiah introduces us to the benefit of doing so. He begins his time of praise by remembering who God is: the great and awesome God. Dwelling upon the attributes of God is a great way to start your time of praise. Nehemiah then reflects upon what God had done: he had kept his covenant promises and revealed his love to his people. Notice how reflecting upon the character of God prepares us to see what he has done when we may have a tendency to reflect upon our negative circumstances. Praise and thanksgiving comprises about 16% of his prayer time.

(2) The Second Focus: Confession & Humility

From the lives of Cain, Moses, and Jonah, we have learned the importance of humility as a deterrent to self-pity. The best way to accomplish this in our prayer life is through confession: acknowledging our sin before the

Lord. His confession progresses from the nation, to his family, to himself. Genuine confession is a restraint to self -pity because it offers the hope of change. We can make things right with the Lord and move forward. We can also take humility with us; acknowledging our failure in the past, and moving forward with God's grace and forgiveness. Confession comprises 28% of his prayer.

(3) The Third Focus: Scripture & the Will of God

More than half of Nehemiah's prayer is a direct quotation of an earlier passage of Scripture. He quotes an earlier promise God had made through Moses to the Israelites. While God does not need to be reminded of his past promises, we do. Nehemiah gains confidence about the will of God for his life by leaning into the Scripture during his prayer time. A.W. Tozier once said, "If God gives you a watch, are you honoring him more by asking him what time it is, or consulting the watch?" Open your Bible to a familiar passage and read it during your prayer time. You are more likely to discern God's will for your life this way than by simply asking for direction. Remarkably, the use of Scripture comprises 50% of Nehemiah's prayer.

(4) The Fourth Focus: The Request

If we pray while we are struggling with self-pity, we tend to bring a complaining spirit to that prayer time. Nehemiah's balanced pattern of praise, confession and Scripture leaves only 14 words for the request — no time for complaining. He makes his request and goes back to work. His request consumes only 6% of his prayer time.

This is a unique pattern and may take some discipline to develop, but as your prayer life parallels Nehemiah's, you will find significant victory over self-pity.

5 Steps to Developing a Praise Journal

The 136th Psalm provides a helpful pattern for developing a personal praise journal. Read the Psalm, purchase a blank journal or open your iPad and get started.

Step 1: Begin with the character of God.

This Psalm begins with the words "Give thanks to the Lord, for he is good." If you are struggling with things for which to give God thanks, make a list of his attributes with biblical verses. Visit biblicalstrategies.com for ideas.

Step 2: Review the works of God.

If you're drawing a blank, then start with creation. The Psalmist focuses on the creative work of God for six verses. The Bible says, "the heavens declare the glory of God." Giving God thanks for creation can prime the pump for more praise.

Step 3: List the protection & provision of God.

The Psalmist remembers how God protected and provided for the Israelites. Make two columns with two headings: "protection and provision." List the ways that God has worked in your past. Be specific. The events listed in Psalm 136 actually happened at a time in history so include the dates if you remember them.

Step 4: Tie it all to the mercy of God.

The phrase "his mercy endures forever" is repeated 25 times in this Psalm. Tie your blessings and difficulties to God's gracious hand. See 2 Corinthians 12:9-10.

Step 5: Recite the goodness of God.

The Psalms were collected to serve as the Hebrew's songbook. The words would have been familiar to the Israelites; they would have sung them in worship. By reciting and reviewing, they remembered God work. Return to your praise journal regularly – not just to add to it, but to review, in order that you can remember.

3 Questions of Bible Study

(1) Observation asks, "What do I see?" Observation is simply gathering all the facts of who, what, where, and when. Careful examination of the facts is the foundation upon which we build accurate interpretation.

(2) Interpretation asks, "What does it mean?" Drawing conclusions based on your study of the facts is the process of interpretation . . . we seek to understand the meaning that the author had in mind.

(3) Application asks, "How should I respond?" Application is the goal of Bible Study. In this final step of the process, we move from the original context to our contemporary one, seeking to know how our interpretation can affect our attitudes and behavior.

Taken from *Unlocking the Scriptures* [168]

9 Questions for Application

- Is there an example for me to follow?
- Is there a sin to avoid?
- Is there a promise to claim?
- Is there a prayer to repeat?
- Is there a command to obey?
- Is there a condition to meet?
- Is there a verse to memorize?
- Is there an error to mark?
- Is there a challenge to face?

Taken from *Living by the Book* [169]

28 Daily Bible Readings for Self-Pity

These readings focus on the love of God, will of God, and glory of God (see pages 39-49). Visit biblicalstrategies.com for additional Bible reading schedules.

DAILY READINGS   DAILY APPLICATION

DWELL UPON THE LOVE OF GOD

Day 1: Psalm 25:1-22

Day 2: Psalm 34:1-24   *As you read these Bible passages*

Day 3: Psalm 86:1-17   *consider: (1) How is God's love*

Day 4: Psalm 103:1-22   *expressed in this passage? (2) In*

Day 5: Psalm 106:1-48   *what ways has God shown his*

Day 6: Isaiah 54:4-14   *love to me personally? (3) How*

Day 7: Romans 5:6-11   *should my attitude/actions*

Day 8: Romans 8:31-37   *change today as I dwell upon*

Day 9: Deut. 7:6-11   *God's love for me?*

Day 10: Luke 15:11-24

Day 11: Ephesians 3:15-19

Day 12: 1 John 4:7-11

Day 13: John 15:9-17

SEEK THE WILL OF GOD

Day 14: 1 John 3:11-18   *As you read these Bible pas-*

Day 15: Romans 12:1-2   *sages consider: (1) How is God's*

Day 16: 1 Thess. 5:12-28   *will defined in this passage? (2)*

Day 17: Psalm 40:1-8   *What choices can I make today*

Day 18: Psalm 143:1-12   *to pursue his will for me?*

Day 19: 1 Thess. 4:1-9

Day 20: 1 John 2:15-17

LIVE FOR THE GLORY OF GOD

Day 21: Psalm 8-9   *As you read these Bible passages*

Day 22: Psalm 19:1-14   *consider: (1) How is God's glory*

Day 23: Psalm 90:1-17   *revealed in this passage? (2)*

Day 24: Isaiah 6:1-7   *What is the response of those*

Day 25: John 11:17-44   *who view God's glory? (3) What*

Day 26: John 12:20-28   *should my response be?*

Day 27: Romans 11:33-36

Day 28: Revelation 4-5

The Scripture Retrieval Method

The Scripture retrieval method is based upon three premises: (1) Scripture provides an excellent *defense* against temptation. This is why the first ten verses listed below are learned in the lie/truth formula to defend against temptation. (2) Scripture provides an excellent *offense* to weaken temptation's appeal. This is why the second ten verses are learned about the character of God and the nature of the Gospel. Loving God well and appreciating the Gospel weakens the draw of temptation. (3) We learn the Scriptures best when we *understand* the words we are memorizing and *apply* them to our real life challenges. For this reason, memory alone is an ineffective means of defending against sin.

Biblical Truths to Combat the Deceiver's Lies

Lie 1: You're all alone. God isn't there when you need him.
Truth: Hebrews 13:5b-6

Lie 2: If God did love you, your life wouldn't be so hard.
Truth: Romans 5:3-4

Lie 3: You keep failing. You'll never have victory over this sin.   Truth: Philippians 1:6; 4:13

Lie 4: If your life was better, you would be happy.
Truth: Philippians 4:11-12

Lie 5: You can't change. That's just the way you are.
Truth: 2 Corinthians 5:17

Lie 6: God is keeping something good from you.
Truth: Psalm 84:10-12

Lie 7: Look at others. See how they have what you don't?
Truth: 2 Corinthians 10:12

Lie 8: No one gave you credit for what you did.
    Truth: James 4:6, 10
Lie 9: You were mistreated/misjudged. You have a right to
    be angry. Truth: 1 Peter 2:21, 23
Lie 10: You don't have the strength to go on. Just give up.
    Truth: Isaiah 40:31

Biblical Promises about God and the Gospel

Promise 1: God is working all things for my good.
    Passage: Romans 8:28
Promise 2: God loves me and enjoys acting on my behalf.
    Passage: Zephaniah 3:17
Promise 3: God will be my help in my time of need.
    Truth: Psalm 121:1, 2
Promise 4: Nothing can separate me from the love of God.
    Passage: Romans 8:35, 37
Promise 5: God is purposefully at work in my life and
    circumstances. Passage: Jeremiah 29:11, 13
Promise 6: God will be with me in my trials. I am not alone.
    Passage: Isaiah 43:2
Promise 7: God strengthens me to do his will.
    Passage: 1 John 5:14, 15
Promise 8: God loves me. I am a part of his family.
    Passage: 1 John 3:1, 2
Promise 9: Having been forgiven, I need not fear God's
    condemnation. Passage: Romans 8:1
Promise 10: God is merciful. He gives me a new start.
    Passage: 1 Peter 1:3-5

Visit biblicalstrategies.com to order these 20 memory verse
cards with helpful commentary on the back of each card.

Walking in the Spirit

The Bible uses the word *walk* to communicate the daily choices we are making. Those choices become habit forming and eventually shape our lives and define our future. As believers, the Holy Spirit empowers our ability to make new choices. This is why Paul wrote, "Walk by the Spirit, and you will not gratify the desires of the flesh" (Gal. 5:16). A practical way to do this is to choose the Spirit's fruit as opposed to your flesh's desires. Look closely at the following two lists. Identify the "desire of the flesh" with which you are most likely struggling (Gal. 5:19-21). Consider which item from the "fruit of the Spirit" list would be the most likely replacement (Gal. 5:22-23).

REPLACEMENT LIST Fruit of the Spirit	DESIRES LIST Works of the Flesh
Love	Sexual immorality
Joy	Impurity
Peace	Lustful pleasures
Patience	Idolatry
Kindness	Sorcery
Goodness	Hostility
Faithfulness	Quarreling
Gentleness	Jealousy
Self-control	Outbursts of anger
	Selfish ambition
	Dissension
	Division
	Envy
	Drunkenness
	Wild parties

(1) Identify the struggle

To identify the struggle, ask good questions around the five W's. *When* are you most likely to be tempted? *What* are the circumstances that lead up to responding with sinful desires? *Who* are you with when you're tempted? *Why* are you susceptible to this temptation – are there underlying motives you haven't considered? *Which* desire from the "works of the flesh" list is your greatest struggle?

(2) Replace the desire with the fruit

Once you have identified the struggle, look to the fruit of the Spirit and indentify its replacement. For example: replace fits of anger with patience, jealousy with joy, selfish ambition with love, hostility with gentleness, and so forth.

(3) Study and apply the truth

Once you've chosen the item from the fruit of the Spirit list, study it. You can use a topical Bible to locate other biblical passages where the word is explained. Develop an understanding using another author's insight.[170] Write a workable definition of the word.[171] Now, apply those definitions to your specific situation. For instance, perhaps you need patience with your kids, peace with your spouse, or love with your fellow employee. Review the definition in advance of the challenge. Imagine various scenarios that could take place, then mentally practice your response.

(4) Repeat the process for permanence

Practice doesn't make perfect, practice makes permanent. As you have practiced giving into the "deeds of the flesh", you have developed those desires into habits. Reversing that order will take time, but by the Spirit's power it is possible. This is why *walking* is an excellent metaphor for how we grow in the Spirit. Step by step we learn new patterns of thinking, choosing and living.

NOTES

1. Tim Keller's commentary on Lewis is helpful. He writes, "C.S. Lewis in *Mere Christianity* makes a brilliant observation about gospel-humility at the very end of his chapter on pride. If we were to meet a truly humble person, Lewis says, we would never come away from meeting them thinking they were humble. They would not be always telling us they were a nobody (because a person who keeps saying they are a nobody is actually a self-obsessed person). The thing we would remember from meeting a truly gospel-humble person is how much they seemed to be totally interested in us. Because the essence of gospel-humility is not thinking more of myself or thinking less of myself, it is thinking of myself less" (http://kellerquotes.com/gospel-humility).

2. Mark 10:45

3. 1 John 3:17

4. Matthew 16:23 reads, "But Jesus turned and said to Peter, [...] 'You aren't thinking the way God thinks but the way humans think'" GWT

5. 1 John 2:6 reads, "Those who say they live in God should live their lives as Jesus did." NLT

6. Romans 8:9, 26, 29

7. Romans 8:11

8. See Galatians 5:16, 18, 25. Four verbs give insight here. Each is associated, directly or indirectly, with the phrase "walk in the Spirit." For further study, see *Just Like Jesus:* *biblical strategies for growing well*, 43-50.

9. This narrative is my imaginative retelling of the Cain and Abel story. Where I have referenced the Scriptures, the narrative is historically accurate. Where there is no biblical reference, I believe it to be a reasonable possibility. The biblical record is found in Genesis 4:1-15.

10. Hebrews 11:5

11. The Genesis text only expresses God approval of Abel's sacrifice; it doesn't say how this approval was revealed. As this is the way that God communicated his approval of Elijah's sacrifice in 1 Kings 18:36-39; it seems reasonable that God might have done something similar with Abel's offering.

12. Genesis 4:7

13. The Samaritan Pentateuch, Septuagint, Syriac, Vulgate, and RSV translations assert that Cain lured Abel into the field so that he could kill him. The act of murder was intentional and premeditated. It was not simply an act of rage.

14. Genesis 4:7

15. Genesis 4:1-2.

16. This was the position Martin Luther held. Note Matthew Henry's comment, "Many suppose that Eve had a conceit that this son was the promised seed, and that therefore she thus triumphed in him, as her words may be read, *I have gotten a man, the* Lord, God-man." Matthew Henry, Matthew Henry's Commentary on the Whole Bible, (Peabody, MA: Hendrickson).

17. Genesis 3:15

18. *Vine's Complete Expository Dictionary of Old and New Testament Words* explains the meaning of Abel's name: "The word represents human 'breath' as a transitory thing. [It also] means something meaningless and purposeless."

19. Hebrews 11:4

20. Genesis 4:4

21. Proverbs 14:6

22. Genesis 4:3-7

23. Taken from the teaching of Ken Collier, Director of *The Wilds*, a summer camp in Brevard, North Carolina.

24. Genesis 4:6

25. Genesis 4:7

26. Romans 6:16, NLT

27. Genesis 4:7

28. Jonah 3:1; John 21:15-17

29. W.E. Vine, *Vine's Expository Dictionary of Old and New Testament Words* (Nashville, TN: Thomas Nelson, 1996), 403-404.

30. Genesis 4:7

31. The Greek word *epithumeo* means to desire or long after. In a positive sense, it means desire as a result of physical needs; in a negative sense, of coveting and lusting after. Spiros Zodhiates, *The Complete Word Study Dictionary* (Chattanooga, TN: AMG Publishers, 1986).

32. Hebrews 11:4, NLT

33. Nicholas Ellen, *With All You Heart: Identifying and Dealing with Idolatrous Lust* (Mustang, OK: Dare 2 Dream Books, 2008).

34. Romans 1:28-31

35. Genesis 4:7

36. This narrative is my imaginative retelling of the account. The historical record is found in Numbers 11.

37. Numbers 11:10

38. Numbers 11:1

39. Numbers 11:33

40. Numbers 11:11-15, *The Message*

41. Numbers 11:16

42. Numbers 11:21-22

43. Exodus 15:23; 17:7

44. Numbers 11:34; 20:13; 21:3

45. Exodus 17:7

46. Numbers 11:34

47. Dennis Cole comments, "The people complained soon after they had seen God's miraculous work in the crossing of the Red Sea and again soon after leaving the place where they had encountered him and entered into a special covenant relationship with him. [...] The text [Num. 11:1] translates literally 'and so the people became like those murmuring evil in the ears of Yahweh.' God had promised goodness and blessing; the people responded with rebellious complaints." R.D. Cole, *The New American Commentary* (Nashville, TN: Broadman & Holman Publishers), 181.

48. Numbers 11:14

49. Numbers 12:3

50. 1 Corinthians 10:11-12

51. Numbers 11:1, 4-5

52. Exodus 2:23-24

53. James 1:14-15

54. Some might argue that a person's desires become so strong that they unconsciously distort memory

and preclude rational decision making. In other words, selective memory really isn't a conscious process. But the Bible holds us accountable for our desires and our thoughts, and offers us the hope that both can be changed. See 2 Corinthians 10:5; Deuteronomy 15:9; Proverbs 15:26; Isaiah 55:7; 59:7.

55. Deuteronomy 8:2-3

56. James 1:16-17

57. Paul affirms this truth when he writes: "a thorn was given me in the flesh, messenger of Satan to harass me, to keep me from becoming conceited. Three times I pleaded with the Lord about this, that it should leave me. But he said to me, 'My grace is sufficient for you, for my power is made perfect in weakness.' Therefore I will boast all the more gladly of my weaknesses, so that the power of Christ may rest upon me. For the sake of Christ, then, I am content with weaknesses, insults, hardships, persecutions, and calamities. For when I am weak, then I am strong" (2 Corinthians 12:7-10).

58. I define emotions as how you *feel* about yourself and your circumstances. Sometimes these feelings can seem so real we are convinced that they confirm the truth. But the Bible teaches that our feelings are prone to change; therefore we are warned to exercise self-control over potentially destructive emotions like unrighteous anger (Ephesians 4:31-32), unmitigated sadness (Ecclesiastes 3:1, 4) or unrestrained fear (Psalm 27:1; Hebrews 13:6).

59. Malachi 3:6

60. Exodus 3:12

61. Deuteronomy 34:10-12

62. Numbers 11:11-14

63. Hebrews 13:6

64. Numbers 11:14

65. 1 Corinthians 10:13, NLT

66. Hebrews 13:5-6

67. Romans 12:4-21; 1 Corinthians 12:12-31

68. John 12:27-34; 14:1-6

69. The phrase "number on foot" communicates the number of men eligible to go to war. When you add in the women and children, a reasonable estimate of their population would be between 1.5 – 2 million people.

70. Numbers 11:21-22

71. Numbers 11:23

72. In *Just like Jesus: biblical strategies for growing well*, I noted that when Jesus became man (Galatians 4:4), he took on the limitations of humankind and lived within those limitations during his few short years on earth. For instance, as a human being he needed sleep (Mark 4:38), while as God he did not (Psalm 121:4). The Bible communicates that Jesus lived within those same limitations *spiritually*. The Scriptures tell us that he endured life's hardships and learned through them (Heb. 5:8); that he grew in favor with God and man despite the latter's sinfulness and imperfect treatment of him throughout his life (Luke 2:48; 4:29; 23:20-25); and that, while he lived and was tempted within those human limitations, he never sinned (Heb. 4:15; 1 John 3:5; 4:2).

73. "You are God Alone" by William McDowell, © 2011.

74. Psalm 139:16

75. 1 Corinthians 4:5

76. Ezekiel 36:26-27; Titus 3:5-6

77. Philippians 4:6; Matthew 6:25-34

78. 1 Corinthians 4:5, Romans 14:1-23

79. 2 Timothy 2:24-26

80. Romans 11:33-34

81. Romans 8:28

82. "In Genesis 41:46 we learn that Joseph was thirty years old when he was made overseer to the king of Egypt. Since he was seventeen when he was sold into slavery, that means he spent thirteen years in Potiphar's house and in prison. We know Joseph was in prison at least 2 years because chapter 40 tells us about the servants of the king whose dreams Joseph interpreted. The first verse of chapter 41 tells us that 2 years passed after that event before the king had the dreams that Joseph was called to interpret" (http://agards-bible-timeline.com).

83. Genesis 50:20

84. This is my imaginative retelling of this account. The historical record is found in Jonah 1-4.

85. Psalm 100:5

86. 1 Peter 5:6; James 4:10

87. Luke 18:9-20

88. Jeremiah 29:11

89. Galatians 1:10

90. In the Biblical record it appears that more men than women struggle with self-pity when they face difficulty or defeat. This has also been the case in my pastoral counseling.

91. Just thinking about *pride* and *grace* bears this out. Imagining a person filled with pride evokes a self-confident demeanor, the image of rights deserved and privileges won. In contrast, envisioning a person in need of grace brings to mind just that: a person in need. The latter recognizes he is impoverished; he realizes he can't bring about the necessary change on his own, and he is grateful for whatever help is extended. See 1 Corinthians 15:9.

92. Jonah 1:17

93. Jonah 3:1

94 Jonah 4:6

95. Job 1:21

96. Job's response to his wife's disparaging comments furthers this idea. His response "shall we receive good from God and shall we not receive disaster?" shows that he believed all of life was a gift, both the good and the bad. He did not believe God's blessings were deserved, but rather gifts received. See Job 2:10.

97. Jonah 3:6-10

98. Jonah 1:3

99. Jonah 1:5

100. Jonah 4:1

101. Jonah 4:1,3,4,9

102. Acts 26:9-11

103. 1 Corinthians 15:9

104. 1 John 3:5, 4:2

105. 1 John 2:6

106. John 7:1-5

107. Mark 14:36

108. Matthew 26:49-50

109. Matthew 26:57-27:56; Mark 14:43-15:47; Luke 22:47-23:49; John 18:12-19:30.

110. Mark 14:37, 50

111. Luke 19:41-44

112. Because self-pity is so closely attached to our feelings, an understanding of love that springs only from feelings will lack the staying power to overcome negativity. Clarifying how we feel due to actions that were taken is essential for change. Moving beyond the subjective feeling to the objective cause is essential. For instance, your spouse may say, "I don't feel loved by you anymore." How much better to say: "When you're angry and sarcastic I don't feel loved by you." Now the feeling has a specific cause that can be addressed accordingly. Feeling loved is a result of the actions that were taken (1 Corinthians 13:4-9) or the promises that were made and kept (Zephaniah 3:17).

113. While the Bible does speak of feelings of compassion, and conveys emotional responses for those we love, those emotions are the expression of one's love, not the cause. This is an important distinction: the commitment doesn't spring forth from the feelings, the feelings spring forth from the commitment or lack thereof. This is evident in the story that Jesus tells about the prodigal son. There was a boy who received his share of the inheritance, took it and spent it in riotous living. When the money ran out, he returned home having lost everything. This is enough to make any father feel bad, but the father is delighted in the boy's return. The Scripture says, "But while he was still a long way off, his father saw him and felt compassion, and ran and embraced him and kissed him." There was no feeling of self-pity on the part of a father who had lost half of his personal equity to his son's careless living. He held no grudge. Had he been dwelling upon the loss of his wealth or his son's disrespect, bitterness would have set in, and he would not have been genuinely joyful at his son's return. The emotion was there at the point of return, because the commitment to love was there throughout. The weakness of a feeling-based love is revealed through the prodigal's older brother. He had no feelings of love for his brother, only disdain for his return. Acting upon those feelings, he refused to join in the homecoming celebration. When his father addressed this, self-pity ran rampant in the older brother's response.

114. Corinthians 13:4-8

115. The world *agape* is translated "love, affectionate regard, goodwill, benevolence." With reference to God's love, it is God's willful direction toward man. It involves God doing what He knows is best for man and not necessarily what man desires. For example, John 3:16 states, "For God so loved the world, that he gave." What did He give? Not what man wanted, but what God knew man needed, i.e., His Son

to bring forgiveness to man. Spiros Zodhiates, *The Complete Word Study Dictionary* (Chattanooga, TN: AMG Publishers, 1986).

116. Romans 5:8, 10

117. John 12:27; Mark 14:36

118. John 15:9

119. Malachi 3:6

120. John 15:9

121. John 15:12-13

122. John 15:12-13

123. Genesis 3:6

124. Romans 8:18-24

125. Luke 22:39-40

126. Luke 2:52; Hebrews 5:8

127. Matthew 16:22

128. Matthew 16:23

129. 1 Corinthians 2:8, 13

130. Hebrews 5:8

131. Mark 14:36

132. In the garden Jesus used the term *Abba* in reference to his father. Most scholars concur that this was a family term similar to *Daddy*. "As concerns the usage of Jesus, the probability is that He employed the word *Abba* . . . particularly in address to God. . . In so doing He applies to God a term which must have sounded familiar and disrespectful to His contemporaries because used in the everyday life of the family. In other words, He uses the simple 'speech of the child to its father.'" G. Kittel, *The Theological Dictionary of the New Testament* (Grand Rapids, MI: Eerdmans, 1964), 6-7.

133. Mark 9:23, 10:27

134. Luke 23:46

135 Matthew 12:40

136. John 12:24

137. John 11:33; 14:1, 27

138. John 12:27-28

139. Luke 22:15

140. John 13:3-5

141. Philippians 2:5-8

142. John 16:7

143. Galatians 5:16

144. Galatians 5:25; Luke 4:1

145. John 14:16, 26

146. Romans 8:10, 11

147. Philippians 4:13

148. John 16:13

149. These three interactions with the Word are covered in detail in *Just Like Jesus: biblical strategies for growing well.*

150. 2 Timothy 3:16-17

151. 2 Peter 1:21

152. 1 John 2:27, NLT

153. Luke 4:1-13

154. James 1:22

155. Galatians 5:16

156. Galatians 5:20, 22

157. ibid.

158. ibid.

159. John 14:26, KJV

160. Romans 8:26-27

161. Psalm 147:6

162. The number 650 does not take into consideration the Psalms, which form a prayer book by themselves. Herbert Lockyer, *All the Prayers of the Bible.*

163. Prayer patterns are discussed in greater detail in *Just Like Jesus: biblical strategies for growing well*, 9-22.

164. Romans 8:11-13

165. Ken Boa, *Vol. 6: Romans. Holman New Testament Commentary* (Nashville, TN: Broadman &

Holman Publishers, 2000), 252.

166. http://www.loc.gov/loc/walls/
jeff1.html

167. Exodus 7:7

168. Hans Finzel, *Unlocking the
Scriptures* (Colorado Springs, CO:
Cook Publishers, 2003), 19.

169. Howard Hendricks, *Living by
the Book* (Chicago, IL: Moody Publishers, 1991), 166.

170. I recommend *A Fruitful Life* by
Jerry Bridges and *A Woman's Walk
with God - Growing in the Fruit of the
Spirit* by Elizabeth George.

171. See *Just Like Jesus: biblical strategies for growing well*, 69-70.

NOTES

NOTES

About the Author

Phil Moser is the author of the Biblical Strategies series. He is a pastor, frequent blogger (philmoser.com) and conference speaker. He holds a degree in Business Management, and earned his Masters of Divinity from The Master's Seminary, Sun Valley, California. He presently serves as the teaching pastor of Fellowship Bible Church in Mullica Hill, New Jersey. He has served as an adjunct professor teaching the Bible, theology, apologetics, homiletics, and counseling in Albania, Korea, Germany, Hungary and Ukraine.

Resources from Biblical Strategies

Just Like Jesus: biblical strategies for growing well

Fighting the Fire: biblical strategies for overcoming anger

Dead End Desire: biblical strategies for overcoming self-pity

Taking Back Time: biblical strategies for overcoming procrastination

Safe in the Storm: biblical strategies for overcoming anxiety

Discerning the Deception: biblical strategies for overcoming sexual temptation

Biblical Strategies
How you get to where God's taking you.
BiblicalStrategies.com

NOTES